TE DUE

W9-BEW-409

AR
5.8
1pt

DISCARD

RECEIVED

AUG 2 8 2000

WALNUT CREEK
SCHOOL DISTRICT

582.16 MEL

C,6 – WCL

YOUNG SCIENTIST CONCEPTS & PROJECTS

TREES

PETER MELLETT

Gareth Stevens Publishing
MILWAUKEE

RECEIVED

AUG 2 8 2000

WALNUT CREEK
SCHOOL DISTRICT

The original publishers would like to thank the following children, and their parents, for modeling in this book — Charlene Da Cova, Anthony Daniels, Laura Harris-Stewart, Lauren Hooper, Mitzi Hooper, Hollie Victoria Howell, Vadim Khramov, Justyna Kucharska, Kevin Loke, Nabil Mehdinejad, Tara Minto. They would also like to thank Steve Hooper Gardens.

For a free color catalog describing Gareth Stevens' list of high-quality books and multimedia programs, call 1-800-542-2595 (USA) or 1-800-461-9120 (Canada). Gareth Stevens Publishing's Fax: (414) 225-0377. See our catalog, too, on the World Wide Web: http://gsinc.com

Library of Congress Cataloging-in-Publication Data

Mellett, P. (Peter), 1946–
Trees / by Peter Mellett.
p. cm. — (Young scientist concepts and projects)
Includes bibliographical references and index.
Summary: Provides an overview of trees, their component parts, how they grow, varieties of trees, and how we use trees and their products. Includes related experiments and projects.
ISBN 0-8368-2087-8 (lib. bdg.)
1. Trees—Juvenile literature.   2. Trees—Experiments—Juvenile literature.
[1. Trees.   2. Trees—Experiments.   3. Experiments.]   I. Title.   II. Series.
QK475.8.M45   1998
582.16—dc21   97-41624

This North American edition first published in 1998 by
Gareth Stevens Publishing
1555 North RiverCenter Drive, Suite 201
Milwaukee, WI 53212 USA

Original edition © 1997 by Anness Publishing Limited.
First published in 1997 by Lorenz Books, an imprint of Anness Publishing Inc., New York, New York. This U.S. edition © 1998 by Gareth Stevens, Inc. Additional end matter © 1998 by Gareth Stevens, Inc.

Managing Editor, Children's Books: Sue Grabham
Editor: Charlotte Evans
Consultant: Michael Chinery
Photographer: Tim Ridley
Stylists: Tim Grabham and Marion Elliot
Designer: Caroline Grimshaw
Picture Researcher: Marion Elliot
Illustrator: Alisa Tingley
Gareth Stevens series editor: Dorothy L. Gibbs
Editorial assistant: Diane Laska

All rights reserved. No part of this book may be reproduced, stored in a retrieval system, or transmitted in any form or by any means, electronic, mechanical, photocopying, recording or otherwise without the prior written permission of the copyright holder.

Printed in the United States of America

1 2 3 4 5 6 7 8 9 02 01 00 99 98

TREES

CONTENTS

PARTS OF A TREE

TREES are plants that grow all around the world, from the frozen arctic to the steamy jungles around the equator. Wherever they grow and whatever their shape, all trees have three things in common – they have roots, leaves, and a single, woody trunk. The part above the trunk is called the crown and is made up of branches, twigs, and leaves. The crown gives each tree its own distinctive shape.

Unlike us, trees grow throughout their lives. Each year, a whole new layer grows under their bark, making them a little thicker. At the same time, roots and twigs grow longer, increasing the tree's spread above and below the ground.

FACT BOX
- The roots of a mature oak cover the same area as a football field.

- A tropical balsa tree can grow 6 feet (1.8 meters) taller in a year, while an arctic Sitka spruce may grow only 1 inch (2.5 centimeters) in a year.

- The first trees (*Archaeopteris*) grew over 350 million years ago.

- The Tasmanian huon pines are the oldest known living trees. Some of them are at least 10,000 years old.

- The tallest living trees are some eucalyptus trees growing in Australia. One was recently measured at over 500 feet (152.4 m) tall.

Leaves
Leaves are where the tree makes its food. Green leaves use sunlight to make sugary sap by joining water from the ground with carbon dioxide gas from the air.

Buds
Buds form at the tips of twigs. They also appear along the sides of twigs and thinner branches. Flowers or new leaves and stems grow from the buds in spring.

Like all trees, this oak has roots, a trunk, branches, twigs, and leaves. It grew from a tiny acorn that sprouted more than 150 years ago. Each year, the girth of its trunk will increase by about 1 inch (2.5 cm), and it will produce up to 50,000 acorns.

Bark

Bark is the woody skin that prevents a tree from drying out. It also protects the tree from attack by animals and fungi. Old bark splits as the tree's branches and trunk grow thicker each year.

Acorn

Root

Branches

The largest branches grow out from the main trunk of the tree. These branches divide into smaller and smaller branches. At the ends of the branches are twigs from which leaves grow. All branches start life as thin twigs when a tree is young.

Seeds

Acorns are the seeds of an oak tree. They fall to the ground where some may sprout and become new oak trees, but most of them rot or are eaten by animals.

Roots

As a seedling develops, its roots grow into the soil. They will support the fully grown tree against the force of the wind. Roots also take in water and nutrients that help the tree grow.

MEASURING A TREE

Bark

Growth ring

You clearly can see the growth rings on the trunk of this old oak tree. Each year, the tree grows a new ring of wood just under the bark.

How can we find out how old or how tall a tree is? How wide is its crown of branches and leaves? When a tree is cut down, you can find out how old it is by counting the growth rings on the stump. There will be one ring for each year of its life. If there are 100 rings, the tree has lived 100 years. To discover more about a living tree, you can measure it in different ways. The problem about measuring trees is that they are far too big to measure with a ruler. It also is unsafe to climb to the top of a tree. The only way to measure a tree is indirectly, without touching it. With the help of a friend, these two projects will help you estimate the height of a tree and the width of its crown.

M A T E R I A L S

You will need: tape measure, yardstick, felt-tip marker.

Measuring a tree's height

1 With the tape measure, measure 21 feet (6.4 m) from the tree. Push the yardstick into the ground there. Lie flat on the ground a yard (meter) from the yardstick.

2 Using one eye, line up the top of the tree with the yardstick and mark that point on the yardstick. The tree's height is 20 times the height of the mark on the yardstick.

M A T E R I A L S

You will need: compass, 8 markers, tape measure, notebook, pencil, graph paper, ruler, colored pencils.

Measuring the tree's crown

1 Using the compass, walk away from the tree toward the north. Ask a friend to call out when you reach the edge of the tree's crown. Place a marker at this point.

2 Repeat step 1 for the other seven main compass directions. Measure the marker distances from the trunk and write them down.

3 Plot your results on graph paper. Measure 1 inch (2.5 cm) on the paper for each yard (meter) on the ground.

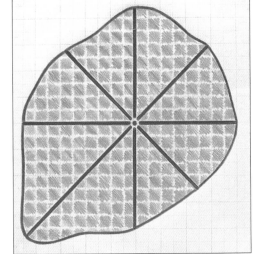

4 Sketch and color in the crown's shape. Then, count the squares and half squares to find its area. Do not count partial squares that are less than half squares.

ROOTS

WHEN you look at a tree, you can see only part of it. Up to one-third lies hidden below the ground. Unseen roots spread out underground as wide as the branches above. These roots anchor the tree in the ground and hold it up against the force of the wind. Main roots are thick and woody, like a tree's branches. They divide toward their ends into smaller and smaller roots. The smallest roots are covered with tiny hairs that have thin skins. These root hairs take up water and nutrients from the soil and pass them on to larger roots and up through the trunk to the leaves. Nutrients help the tree grow strong and healthy.

Gale-force winds have snapped off this beech tree's main roots and blown it over. You can see some of the shallow roots that grew near the surface of the ground.

Shallow roots
Trees grow shallow roots where the soil is poor. All the nutrients lie in a thin, top layer of the soil.

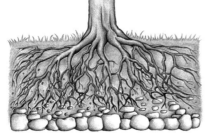

Deeper roots
Trees grow deeper roots in rich soil. Most of the roots, however, still grow in a wide area near the surface.

The banyan tree of India grows roots to support its spreading branches. Pillar roots grow down from the lower branches and take root in the ground. They help the tree spread out over a wide area.

Many giant rain forest trees are over 500 feet (152 m) tall, but their roots grow near the surface. To keep from falling over, the trees have wedge-shaped buttress roots growing up the sides of their trunks.

Mangrove trees grow in soft river mud. Their long slender trunks are supported by prop roots growing out of the trunk. Prop roots work like a tent's ropes to anchor the tree.

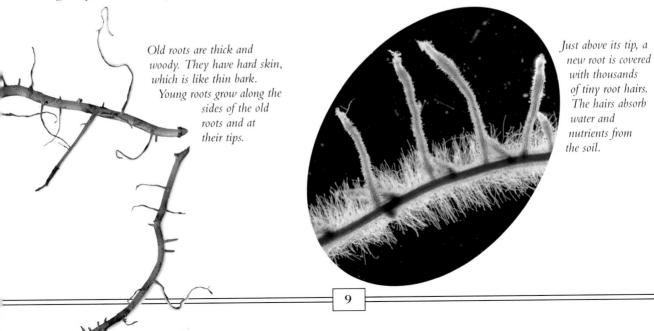

Old roots are thick and woody. They have hard skin, which is like thin bark. Young roots grow along the sides of the old roots and at their tips.

Just above its tip, a new root is covered with thousands of tiny root hairs. The hairs absorb water and nutrients from the soil.

PUMPING WATER

Acting like natural pumps, all trees draw water from deep beneath the ground up into their leaves. Many trees are over 150 feet (45 m) tall and pump hundreds of gallons (liters) of water a day. People can draw up liquids through a straw, but trees cannot do that. Instead, trees use a method called osmosis to force water upward. Osmosis works because there is a difference in the concentration of the sap, or juice, inside the roots and the water in the ground. Sap is more concentrated than groundwater because it contains large amounts of sugary substances. Groundwater contains only tiny amounts of dissolved nutrients. Osmosis forces water from the soil (where concentration is low) into the root (where concentration is high) through tiny holes in the root skin. Tough-walled tubes carry the water up the trunk and into the leaves. The water evaporates from the leaves through tiny holes. As it evaporates, more water moves up to take its place.

To find out how difficult it is to draw up water, carefully join straws with tape. The longer the straw, the more difficult it is for you to draw up the drink. The best mechanical pumps can pump only about 32 feet (10 m).

M A T E R I A L S

You will need: cutting board, peeler, smooth potato, knife, teaspoon, 2 shallow dishes, water, sugar.

How osmosis works

1 Using a cutting board to protect your work surface, carefully peel a smooth potato that is about 4 inches (10 cm) long and 2 inches (5 cm) across.

2 Cut the peeled potato in half and slice off the rounded ends. You will now have two round potato slices. Each slice should be about 1 inch (2.5 cm) thick.

You will need: celery stalk with leaves, knife, clear glass, water, food coloring.

How water travels up a stem

Trees and other plants move water upward through tubes called xylem vessels. You can see these tubes in celery. Cut ½ inch (1.3 cm) from the end of a stalk of celery. Put the celery into a glass of colored water and let it sit for one day.

Xylem vessel

You can see the colored water in the xylem tubes of the celery. Cut across the bottom of the stem for a better view.

3 Use a teaspoon to scoop out a hollow in each potato slice. Place each slice in its own shallow dish. Fill each dish with water to about a ½-inch (1.3-cm) depth.

4 Half fill both hollows with water. Add ½ teaspoon (2.5 milliliters) of sugar to one hollow. Cover the dishes and let them sit for one day. *(Dye added here to make water visible.)*

5 The level of liquid in the sugary hollow has risen. Osmosis has made more water move into this potato from the dish. The level in the other potato has not risen.

TRUNKS AND BARK

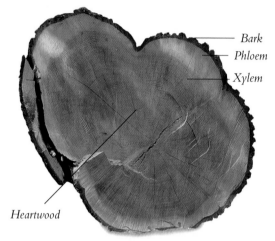

Bark —
Phloem —
Xylem —

Heartwood

Bark protects the living inner part of the tree. The phloem, or inner bark, carries food. The xylem, or inner wood, carries water from the roots to the leaves. The central part of the trunk is dead heartwood.

BARK is the woody skin that covers a tree. It prevents the tree from drying out and also helps protect against attack by animals and fungi. Bark can be thin and smooth or thick and knobby, depending on the type of tree and its age. Young trees have smooth bark on their trunks and branches. Old bark stretches and cracks or peels as a tree grows thicker each year. Just underneath the bark is a delicate layer called the phloem. Trees make their own food that travels around in the phloem. If bark is damaged all around a tree trunk, the flow of food stops and the tree dies.

How bark ages
The bark of a young eucalyptus tree *(left)* is smooth and thin. As the tree grows, more and more layers of bark build up from the inside. The bark of an old eucalyptus tree *(right)* is deeply cracked and wrinkled. Old layers of bark on the outside split as new layers on the inside push outward.

12

Under attack

Deer and other woodland animals chew bark when other food is scarce. Harmful insects or fungi can enter through these wounds, causing disease and more damage to the tree.

Insects and larvae

Stag beetles and other insects lay their eggs under the bark. The eggs hatch into soft-bodied grubs, which eat deeper into the wood with their powerful jaws.

The presence of a woodpecker shows that this tree is unhealthy. The bird pecks at loose bark to search for insects living underneath it.

This ancient willow tree is hollow because the dead heartwood has rotted away. Firm bark still protects the phloem and the xylem layers, so the tree continues to live and grow.

LOOKING AT BARK

You will need: field guide, magnifying glass, binoculars.

DIFFERENT trees have different kinds of bark. A massive beech tree has smooth, thin bark that is about ½ inch (1.3 cm) thick. A redwood tree of the same size has hairy, fibrous bark that is up to 6 inches (15 cm) thick. Many conifers, such as pines and spruces, have bark that flakes off in small pieces. The appearance of the bark can help you decide what species, or type, a tree is. It also can tell you how old a tree is. Young trees have smooth, thin bark that cracks and wrinkles as the tree matures. If you look closely at the bark, you can discover many clues about its life. For example, plants and fungi, both large and small, may be clinging to the surface. Many different kinds of insects and other tiny creatures might be hiding inside cracks and holes. Choose a tree and identify it using a field guide. Then, see what you can find out about your tree by becoming a bark detective!

Become a bark detective

1 Bark does not stretch. It cracks and peels as a tree grows. Use a magnifying glass to search in the cracks, during spring and summer, for tiny insects and other creatures.

2 If you look under loose bark on rotten wood, you might find white threads, called hyphae. These threads are part of a fungus. They are slowly digesting the dead wood.

3 The bark has fallen away from this dead tree revealing the holes chewed in it by beetle grubs. Some grubs live under the bark for several years.

Bark rubbing
Make a collection of bark patterns to take home. Ask a friend to hold a sheet of paper steady against the bark of a tree. Rub the side of a crayon over the paper with long, even strokes. Write the name of the tree beside each rubbing.

You will need: paper, crayon.

Red oak

Horse chestnut

You could make a special book to display your rubbings. Punch holes into pieces of colored cardboard and link them together with ribbon. Paste your rubbings onto each page. You could include a silhouette of each tree as well. Remember to label each page with the name of the tree.

4 Where the bark is damp, you will find powdery green patches, which are millions of microscopic plants called algae. They live side by side on the bark's surface.

5 Look at the upper branches with binoculars. You may find signs of squirrels and other animals. They strip away soft bark, often causing branches to die and drop off.

NEEDLES AND LEAVES

WHICH species, or types, of trees grow near your home? Are they oaks, maples, eucalyptus, acacias, or pines? There are thousands of different species, but most belong to just two main groups – coniferous, or conifer trees, and broad-leaved trees. Conifers, such as pines, firs, and spruces, have needlelike leaves. They grow their seeds inside cones, not flowers. Most conifers are evergreen and are covered with leaves all year round. Broad-leaved trees, such as oaks, birches, and maples, have broad, flat leaves. In tropical climates, most broad-leaved trees are evergreen and grow new leaves steadily as older ones fall away. In colder climates, most broad-leaved trees are deciduous and lose all their leaves in the fall. Broad-leaved trees have flowers and grow their seeds inside fruits, such as nuts and berries.

Conifers, such as pines and spruces, are decorated as Christmas trees, a tradition that spread from Germany. Originally, their evergreen branches were seen as a symbol of hope for new life in the spring.

Evergreen holly
Holly is a broad-leaved evergreen. Its leaves are thick, so they are not damaged by freezing winter weather. A waxy coating keeps the leaves from drying out when water is scarce.

You can see the light shining through this maple leaf. The leaves of deciduous, broad-leaved trees usually are much thinner than evergreen leaves.

The seasons

Young leaf

Spring
The warmth of spring makes the rolled-up leaves of these birch trees burst from their buds. The leaves will grow quickly.

Mature leaf

Summer
In summer, the birch has a dense canopy of mature leaves. They catch the sunlight for photosynthesis.

Dying leaf

Fall
In the fall, all the food flows from the leaves into stems and roots. The leaves turn yellow and fall to the ground.

Winter
All through the cold, dark winter months, deciduous trees are like hibernating animals. Sap hardly moves at all, and growth stops. The tree awaits the arrival of spring.

FROM BUD TO LEAF

Folded leaf

Bud scale

Short stem

This bud is almost ready to burst open. The tough bud scales protect the curled-up leaves inside.

Look closely at trees in winter, and you will see that they are not completely bare. Each twig has buds along its sides and at its tip. Buds have protective skins with tiny immature leaves and stems curled up inside. When spring sunshine warms the trees, buds begin to grow and swell. Finally, the buds burst open, and small leaves emerge. Leaves contain pipes called veins. Water pumps into these veins, making the leaves stiffen and flatten as they grow to full size. To help identify trees, you can make a labeled collection of dried leaves. You also can make rubbings from leaves in the same way you made bark rubbings.

Looking at branches
Wind sometimes rips young branches from trees. If you find one, place it in water and study the branch. You will find that it has buds and leaves at different stages of development.

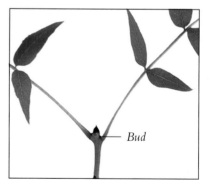

Bud

At the top of this ash twig, between two leaves, there is an unopened bud. It contains tiny leaves and a shoot that will grow in spring and make the twig longer.

Leaf pressings

You will need: gloves, leaves, paper towels, heavy books, glue, notebook, field guide, pencil.

1 To start your leaf collection, you can pick up fallen leaves or cut fresh ones. Wear gloves to protect your hands and make sure you have permission to cut fresh leaves.

2 To dry and flatten your leaves, place sheets of paper towels between the pages of large, heavy books. Lay your leaves out on the paper towels on one side only.

4 Wait at least one month until the leaves are flat and dry. Glue them into your notebook or onto sheets of thick paper made into a book. Use a field guide to identify each leaf. Write the name of the leaf next to it in the book.

Pressed leaves keep their shape and can last forever if they are kept dry.

3 When you have laid out all your leaves, close the books and pile them on top of each other. Put more books on top of the pile. Make sure the pile cannot fall over and will not be disturbed. The weight of the books presses the leaves flat while the paper towels absorb moisture.

LIVING PROCESSES

Just like you, trees are living things. You have to eat to stay alive and grow, but trees and other plants do not have to take in food. They make their own, using water from the ground and carbon dioxide gas from the air. Leaves contain a green substance, called chlorophyll, that traps the energy from sunlight. The trapped energy joins water and carbon dioxide to make oxygen and sugary glucose. This whole process is called photosynthesis. Trees use glucose to make new materials and supply energy for growth. Oxygen escapes back into the air, making the air healthy for people and animals to breathe.

Trees spread their leaves as wide as possible to absorb as much energy as they can from sunlight. They use the energy to make sugary glucose.

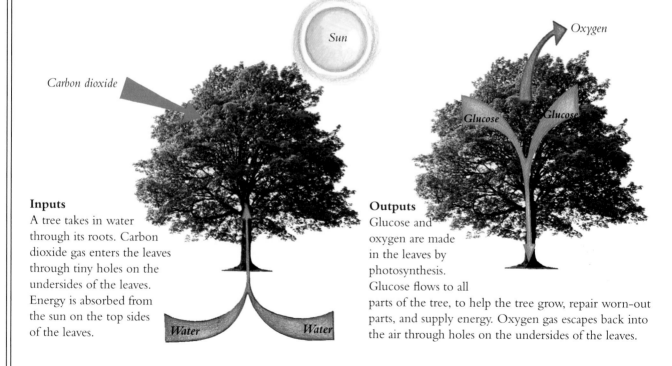

Inputs
A tree takes in water through its roots. Carbon dioxide gas enters the leaves through tiny holes on the undersides of the leaves. Energy is absorbed from the sun on the top sides of the leaves.

Outputs
Glucose and oxygen are made in the leaves by photosynthesis. Glucose flows to all parts of the tree, to help the tree grow, repair worn-out parts, and supply energy. Oxygen gas escapes back into the air through holes on the undersides of the leaves.

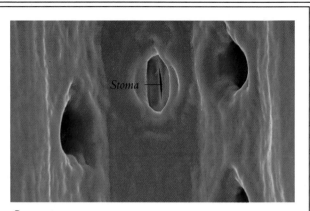

Stomata

Gases flow in and out of leaves through microscopic holes called stomata (one hole is called a stoma). The stomata shown here have been magnified about 200 times so you can see them.

Vein

Veins

Liquids flow in and out of leaves through pipes called veins. On the underside of a leaf, you can see that the veins also act like ribs that help to stiffen the leaf and keep it flat.

Photosynthesis

Photosynthesis happens near the top surface of a leaf where sunlight is strongest.

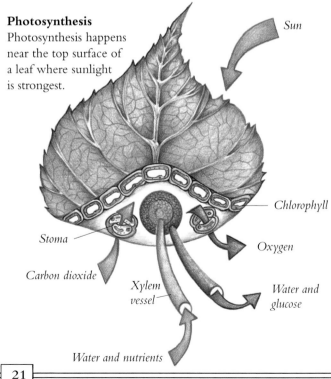

FACT BOX

• If photosynthesis stops, so would all life on earth, because all animals either eat plants or eat other animals that live on plants. The oxygen released through photosynthesis is the source of all oxygen in our atmosphere.

• The skin around a leaf cell is less than $1/1,000$ inch (.03 millimeters) thick.

• Breathing air and burning fuel use up oxygen and produce carbon dioxide. It takes four large trees all day to replace the oxygen used by a car driven for one hour.

LIGHT AND WATER

Trees must have light to live. Without light, they cannot use photosynthesis to make their own food. Look at a leaf, and you will see that the top side usually is greener than the underside. It is because there is more chlorophyll on top where the light is strongest. In shady forests, young trees race each other to reach the light above. They change direction as they grow, avoiding obstacles that block the light.

Warm sunshine makes water evaporate from leaves in the same way that wet clothes dry on the clothesline. Water moves up from the roots and into the leaves. Here, it is changed from a liquid into an invisible gas, called water vapor, and escapes through holes in the leaves. This process is called transpiration.

These are trees in a tropical rain forest. They pass millions of gallons (liters) of water vapor into the air each day. The vapor forms thick clouds of tiny water droplets above the forest.

M A T E R I A L S

Transpiration at work

You will need: clear plastic bag, yarn.

1 In a shady spot, find some leaves at the end of a branch you can reach easily. Put the plastic bag over the leaves and tie the neck of the bag around the branch with yarn.

2 Next morning, you should find droplets of water on the inside of the bag. The leaves have given off water vapor, which has cooled and turned back into liquid water.

Searching for the light

1 Watch a plant search for light as it grows by making a maze. Cut a hole in one end of a shoe box. Cut 8 pieces of black cardboard (4 wide, 4 narrow).

2 Tape the cardboard pieces inside the box (as shown). Paint the insides of the box and lid black to stop light coming through the hole from being reflected inside the box.

3 Plant a bean in a small pot of compost. Water the soil each day to keep it moist but not wet. Some days, water may not be necessary.

4 When the plant has a shoot, stand it in the bottom of your maze. Close the lid tightly and place the maze in a sunny spot. Once a day, remove the lid to see if the seedling needs watering.

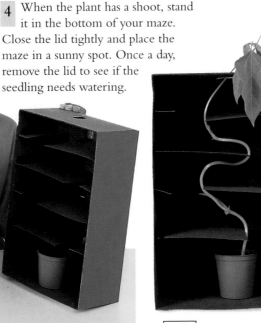

The plant will find its way through the maze as it steadily moves toward the light. Eventually, it will poke out through the hole at the top of the shoe box.

M A T E R I A L S

You will need: shoe box, scissors, stiff black cardboard, tape, black paint, paintbrush, small flowerpot, compost, runner bean, watering can, water.

POLLINATION

Wind pollination
Shake a hazel catkin, and it can scatter over 2 million pollen grains into the air. By chance, the wind may carry some away to the female flowers.

ALL trees grow from seeds. Even a mighty redwood, 250 feet (76 m) high, starts life from a seed the size of your fingernail. There are two ways that trees make seeds – either inside cones or inside flowers. Cone-bearing trees include pines and firs. Flowering trees include oaks and maples. To make seeds, trees have male parts and female parts. In spring, the female parts contain tiny unripe seeds called ovules, while the male parts make grains of dustlike pollen. Pollen must join with the ovules before they can grow into ripe seeds. The male and female parts may be on the same tree or on separate trees far apart from one another. The way pollen travels from the male parts to the female parts is called pollination.

Insect pollination
While a bee feeds on the sugary nectar made by an apple blossom, its body becomes coated with sticky pollen. As it moves to the next flower, it pollinates the female parts. Many trees use flowers to attract insects to spread their pollen.

Bird pollination
This Costa Rican hummingbird pollinates flowers with its long beak as it probes for nectar. Some flowers have special shapes, colors, and nectar to attract particular sorts of animals, such as bats and birds.

How a cedar cone develops

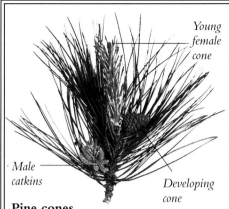

In the fall, cedar trees grow tiny female cones containing ovules. After pollination, when the ovules are fertilized, the female cones start to swell and turn hard.

Pine cones

In early summer, pine trees grow tiny female cones containing ovules. Yellow catkins, or male cones, make pollen that scatters into the air. Later, the male parts shrivel away, and the female cones start to swell and ripen.

Young female cone

Male catkins

Developing cone

As the female cone matures, the scales become woody and change color from green to brown. Cones can take up to three years to mature.

When a cone is mature, the top breaks up and the scales fall to the ground. The cone may take years to disintegrate. All that is left is the central axial on the tree.

The seeds are released as the scales fall. The seeds have papery wings to help them fly far away from the parent tree.

FROM FLOWER TO FRUIT

How many fruits can you think of that grow on trees? Obvious examples include apples, oranges, plums, and pears. They have juicy flesh with seeds buried deep inside. The seeds grew from tiny ovules fertilized by pollen. Most of the fleshy part grew from the ovary wall that surrounded the ovules. Winged sycamore seeds, shiny chestnut conkers, and hard walnuts grow in the same way. They are called fruits, too. Fruits grow on trees that use flowers to reproduce. The seeds are wrapped up inside a container, the fruit, that protects the developing seeds until they are ripe and ready to be spread by the wind or animals. Cones that grow on pines, firs, and spruces are not fruits. Each seed grows loose, because it is tucked between the scales of a cone.

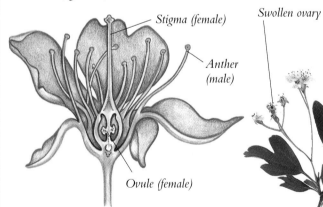

Flowers, such as this elder blossom, are a specialized part of the plant. They develop into fruits and seeds.

Flowers, fruits, and seeds

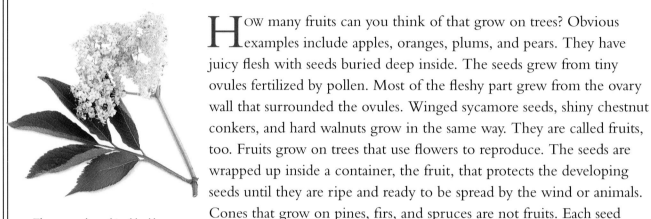

Stigma (female)

Anther (male)

Ovule (female)

Swollen ovary

Flower

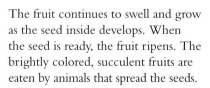

This diagram shows a flower cut in half. Pollen, made by the anthers, lands on the stigma and moves down to the ovary where it fertilizes the ovule.

After fertilization, the flower's petals drop off. The ovary swells to form a fruit. The fertilized ovule inside becomes a seed containing a tiny plant, the embryo, and a store of food.

The fruit continues to swell and grow as the seed inside develops. When the seed is ready, the fruit ripens. The brightly colored, succulent fruits are eaten by animals that spread the seeds.

Seed

Pit

Plums are a type of fruit called a drupe. They have juicy flesh and a single hard pit that contains the seed. Peaches and cherries are drupes, too.

Oranges are fleshy, brightly colored citrus fruits with a strong smell and many seeds. Lemons and limes also are citrus fruits.

Apple blossoms bloom in early spring. Apples have lots of seeds, called pips, inside a core. Some apples turn red as they ripen.

Seed

Seed

A walnut is a drupe, but, on the tree, it is covered by a tough green skin instead of juicy flesh. The seed is inside the hard, woody shell.

When you eat a fruit, such as a juicy apple, be sure to look out for the seeds.

FRUITS AND SEEDS

THERE are many different kinds of fruits. Some fruits are soft, such as apples and oranges, and others are hard, such as acorns and walnuts. Even tough little hawthorn berries and sycamore wings are fruits. We call them fruits because they all have seeds protected inside a container. The container may be the soft flesh of a plum or the hard shell of a hazelnut. Hard or soft, small or large, all fruits contain seeds. You can try to find the seeds hidden inside different fruits. Some examples are given here. If you want to try others, it is safest to use edible fruits bought at your local store.

MATERIALS

You will need: cutting board, sharp knife, tweezers, magnifying glass, apple, orange, apricot, plum, lemon, hazelnut, nutcracker, scissors.

Looking at apple seeds

1 Using a cutting board and a sharp knife, cut open an apple. You will find several brown seeds, or pips, in the center. Use tweezers to remove as many of these seeds as you want.

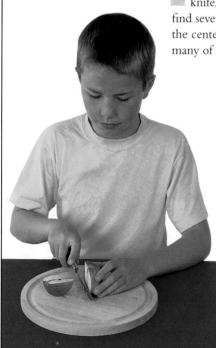

Apple seed

2 With tweezers, carefully remove the soft outer skin of a seed. Underneath the skin, you will find a slippery white seed. Treat it carefully – it is very delicate.

3 Look through a magnifying glass to see the cotyledon and embryo (at the tip). The cotyledon provides food for the embryo, which will grow into a new root and shoot.

Orange

Apricot

Plum

Lemon

Apple

Soft fruits

These fruits are soft, fleshy, and sweet. Like most fruits, they have grown from the ovaries inside female flowers. Open any fruit, and you will find seeds inside.

Looking inside a nut

1 Nuts are fruits that have their seeds inside a hard container. Carefully crack open a hazelnut with a nutcracker and look for the seed (nut kernel) inside.

2 Use scissors to scrape off the dark outer skin of the kernel. Then separate the white hazelnut into two halves. Look at them through a magnifying glass.

3 Inside the nut is a tiny embryo. This part grows into roots and a stem. The two larger parts are the cotyledons, which supply energy for the sprouting seed to grow.

SCATTERING SEEDS

THE best place for many young animals to grow up is close to their parents. The adults protect their young and provide them with food and shelter. However, the best place for a young tree to grow up is as far away as possible from adult trees and from other seeds. Seeds that sprout beneath other trees will not grow strong and healthy. They are sheltered from the light and have to share precious water and nutrients. To give their offspring a good start in life, many trees disperse, or scatter, their seeds far and wide. There are many different ways of dispersing seeds, and the shape and design of a tree's fruit reflect these different methods.

Gyrocopter
Make a model maple seed, or gyrocopter. Cut one-third of a strip of paper in half lengthwise. Fold the cut ends back *(as shown)*. Attach a paper clip at the bottom. What happens when you let it fall?

Fruit

Gyrocopter

Winged seeds
Maple trees have winged fruits growing in pairs. One seed is attached to each wing.

When the seeds are ripe, the fruit falls from the tree. The wings spin like the blades of a helicopter, slowing it down and carrying it far away in a strong wind.

On the ground, the fruit dries out and splits in two.

Animal carriers

Animals, such as this orangutan, enjoy sweet fleshy fruits. They eat the flesh and then throw away the seeds, often far away from where they picked the fruit.

Bird carriers

Some seeds with hard coatings pass unchanged through fruit-eating birds and bats. They finally might emerge many miles (kilometers) away. The seeds land on the ground wrapped in nutrients!

Carried by water

Coconuts float on water. They grow on palm trees that drop their fruits into rivers or the sea. Some young palms sprout thousands of miles away from where the coconut dropped.

You will find some trees growing in very strange places. This pine tree may have grown from a seed that was carried in the wind or dropped by a bird.

GERMINATION

M A T E R I A L S

You will need: gloves, flowerpot with 5-inch (12.5-cm) diameter, compost, acorns or another tree's seeds, trowel, watering can, water.

WHEN a seed begins to grow, we say that it has germinated. Germination starts when warmth and moisture swell the seed and split its skin. A tiny root grows downward, and a thin shoot pushes up toward the light. The root and the shoot have grown from the smallest part of the seed, called the embryo. Food energy for growth comes from the largest parts, which are called the cotyledons. This project will show you how to germinate a seed and help it grow into a tree. You also can germinate beans in a glass jar and see that, whichever way up you place the seed, the root will grow down and the shoot will grow up.

Germinate an acorn

1 Wearing gloves, fill a flowerpot with compost. Bury several acorns, or other tree seeds, just beneath the surface. Put the pot in a warm place and keep the soil moist.

2 This acorn has germinated. The brown root has started to grow downward into the soil, and the green shoot has started to grow toward the light.

3 When a tiny tree starts to grow by itself, it is called a seedling. It needs light and regular watering to grow well. Do not soak the soil with water or the roots will rot and die.

5 This young oak tree is called a sapling and is about ten years old. You and your friends may have grown tree seedlings and planted them at your school. You do not have to grow your trees from seeds. You can save time by buying seedlings at tree nurseries. Germinating a seed takes about two months.

4 Your seedling should grow rapidly for a few weeks and then stop. During winter, it will need very little water. Next spring, you can plant it outside. Have an adult help you choose a good spot. Be careful not to disturb the roots when you transplant the seedling.

How a seed grows

M A T E R I A L S

You will need: glass jar, blotting paper or newspaper, fava bean or runner bean seed, water.

1 Pack a glass jar with blotting paper. Push a bean seed down between the paper and the glass. Add water, 1 inch (2.5 cm) deep. Keep the jar in a light, warm place.

2 When the seed germinates, you can see the root growing downward. Turn the jar so that the root points to the right. What do you think will happen?

The root has changed direction to grow downward again.

CONIFER FORESTS

Forests of conifers grow in a band across northern North America, Europe, and Asia.

DIFFERENT kinds of trees grow naturally in different parts of the world. Where they grow depends mainly on the climate. Evergreen conifer trees, such as pines and firs, usually grow where the climate is cold. Long snowy winters are followed by short cool summers with moderate amounts of rain. The trees often grow close together, shutting out the light and making it difficult for some plants to grow there. A forest is a community of many different plants and animals all living together. All these living things depend on each other, and it takes many centuries for a natural forest to grow.

Growth of a forest

Forests spread very slowly in a series of steps called a succession. Thousands of years ago, simple plants, such as lichens and mosses, lived on bare rock. Shallow soil gradually formed as they lived and died, then rotted away.

Grasses and small plants, such as the arctic willow, then covered the ground. Centuries of growth, death, and decomposition steadily made the soil deeper. Conditions became suitable for shrubs, such as heather, and small trees to grow.

When the soil became deep enough to support trees, young conifers started to grow. Their fallen leaves rotted slowly making the soil acidic. Ferns sprang up in the gaps between the trees. If left alone, this area would have developed into a forest.

In a conifer forest

Hemlocks, cypresses, and giant redwoods grow in the North American forests. Woodpeckers and chipmunks search for insects and seeds in the trees. Ferns grow on the gloomy forest floor. Moose and beavers live in lakes, and black bears scavenge for food to eat.

Needles and scales

All conifers have either needlelike leaves or scalelike leaves. Sitka spruce trees have needle-like leaves that grow in clusters. Cypress trees have needlelike young leaves and flattened, scalelike adult leaves.

Redwood

Pine

Sitka spruce

Cypress

TEMPERATE FORESTS

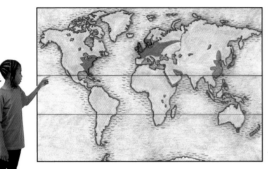

Large temperate forests are found in North America, Europe, Asia, and Australia.

BROAD-LEAVED, deciduous trees, such as oak, ash, and maple, grow in temperate climates away from the hot, dry tropics or the snowy lands of the arctic. The weather is warm and moist, with warm, wet summers followed by short, cold winters. A natural deciduous forest in summer is full of life. There are many more kinds of trees than in a northern coniferous forest. Sunlight pours down through gaps in the canopy, helping flowers, grasses, and bushes grow. All these plants provide food and shelter for a huge variety of creatures.

Simple leaves
Broad-leaved trees have either simple leaves or compound leaves. These three leaves all are simple leaves. Each leaf grows in one piece at the end of its own stalk.

Oak

Common beech

Poplar

In a temperate forest

Beech, ash, and oak grow in this European forest. Squirrels and birds live in the trees. Bluebells, wood anemones, and badgers live on the forest floor. Worms and moles burrow underground. Larger animals include deer, and there even may be wild pigs and brown bears.

Compound leaves

Compound leaves are made up of several small leaflets joined to a single stalk. The leaflets may be arranged along each side of the stalk, or they all may be attached to one point.

Laburnum

Horse chestnut

False acacia

LIFE IN A TREE

AVE you ever walked through a forest in summer? You probably saw hundreds of trees but did not notice the thousands of animals living in them. Woodland creatures usually are very secretive. Small animals are caught and eaten if they do not hide carefully. Larger animals scare away their food if they are noisy. You may not spot the animals themselves, but you often can find the clues they leave behind. Why not spend an afternoon with some friends being nature detectives? The best place to visit is mixed woodland where there are deciduous broad-leaved trees as well as evergreen conifers. Do not forget to take along an adult to carry the sandwiches and keep you safe.

M A T E R I A L S

You will need: field guide, large sheet of paper or cloth, paintbrush, clear jars and boxes, magnifying glass, notebook, pencil.

Become a nature detective

1 On the ground, you may find signs of feeding. These signs include gnawed pine cones and half-eaten nuts and fruits. A field guide will suggest the animals responsible.

2 Look for round holes in dead or dying trees. A woodpecker makes its nest by chipping its way into a hollow tree. Later on, the nest often is used by other birds or animals.

3 This tree is dead and is losing its bark. The wood is soft because it is rotting. Birds and small animals dig holes in the trunk as they search for insects to eat.

Creature time

1 See how many insects you can find living up a tree. You do not have to climb up – simply spread a large sheet of paper or a cloth under a low leafy branch.

2 Shake the branch with short, quick movements. Insects and other small creatures will fall onto your sheet.

3 Before they can scurry away, use your paintbrush to sweep each creature into a clear jar or box.

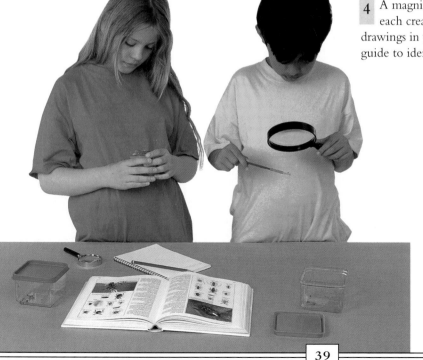

4 A magnifying glass will help you see each creature more clearly. Make drawings in your notebook. Use a field guide to identify each creature.

5 When you have finished, release your captives near the foot of the tree where you found them. They will crawl back up the trunk and carry on with their lives.

TROPICAL TREES

Tropical rain forests grow in South America, Africa, Asia, and Australia.

TROPICAL countries lie close to the equator. The weather is hot, and daylight lasts for 12 hours most of the year. Rain forests grow in tropical regions where heavy rain falls almost continuously. Trees and other plants grow all year round to make a dense jungle that bursts with life. Some other tropical countries have very little rainfall. The sun beats down on barren soil that is dry and sandy. Only a few palms and other specially adapted trees can grow well. They store water in their trunks and roots, and they have long, thin leaves that lose water very slowly.

Drip-tip leaves
Many rain forest trees have deeply grooved leaves with downward pointing drip-tips at the ends. Drip-tips quickly drain rainwater away and prevent leaves from sagging on their stalks.

Rain forest canopy
The trees grow tightly packed together in this rain forest in Cameroon, Central Africa. Seen from the air, the treetops join to make a dense layer called the canopy. The canopy is 100 to 150 feet (30 to 45 m) above the ground.

Life in a rain forest

Many species of trees and climbing plants live in the Amazon rain forest of South America. Most animals, such as frogs, monkeys, sloths, snakes, leopards, and brightly colored birds, live high in the canopy where there is plenty of light, warmth, and food. Dense rotting vegetation covers the ground, providing food for fungi and insects.

Palm trees

Palms are unlike other trees. A palm's stem is not made from layers of wood but from long bundles held side by side. There are no branches. Its leaves are thin and very long and sprout together from the top of the stem.

These palm trees are growing in the Seychelles, a group of islands in the Indian Ocean. They grew from coconuts carried by the sea and washed up on the beach. Rain falls for only two months a year, so forests cannot grow in this sort of climate.

SAVANNA WOODLAND

Tropical grasslands are found in South America, Africa, Asia, and Australia.

SAVANNA is a dry, tropical area. For as far as you can see, the ground is covered with an endless layer of dry grass. There are occasional low shrubs and bushes. Trees grow alone or in widely spaced small groups. Forests cannot grow because the dry season lasts for most of the year. The trees that do grow here are species that can survive for a long time without water. Rain falls for two or three months when seeds germinate, the grass turns green, and flowers bloom. Trees and other plants store water in their roots and stems to last them through the dry months to come.

Drought defenses
Euphorbia trees have small leaves to help cut down on water loss due to evaporation. They also have an unpleasant tasting sap that helps protect the plant from being eaten by hungry animals.

Koalas
Koalas live in dry savanna woodlands in eastern Australia. They eat a constant diet of eucalyptus leaves. Eucalyptus trees originally came from Australia but now exist worldwide. They grow very fast, even in dry conditions.

Life on the savanna

The African savanna is dotted with drought-resistant trees, such as baobabs, or bottle trees, and acacias. Herds of zebra, antelope, and gazelles feed on the grass, while taller giraffes and elephants can reach up into the trees and strip the branches of their leaves. Dung beetles clear up the animal droppings, while vultures look out for a carcass left by a lion, and lizards search for insects.

Thorn trees

Acacias are very common on the African savanna. They also are called thorn trees because of the sharp spines that grow among the leaves. Despite their prickles, many animals rely on acacia leaves for food. Acacias bloom in the wet season.

Storing water

Baobabs have roots that spread out over a wide area. During the rainy season, the trees collect water and store it in their spongy trunks. The distance around a baobab's trunk can be almost as much as its height.

SWAMPS

SWAMPS are places where the ground is permanently waterlogged. The muddy ground is covered with a layer of water for much of the time. There are two kinds of swamps – freshwater and saltwater. Freshwater swamps are found in flat low-lying places. Water from streams and rain flows away very slowly. Saltwater swamps are found in muddy river estuaries close to the sea. The tide flows in and out twice a day, drowning the flat riverbanks with seawater. Most trees cannot survive in swamps because they need fresh water and air around their roots. Some swamps are full of trees that use special methods to survive.

Mangroves growing at the estuary of a river in Australia. Their roots are revealed at low tide.

FACT BOX

• The only trees that can grow in salty water are some types of mangroves. Their seeds start to grow while they still are attached to the tree. When the seeds drop into the mud, they quickly put down roots so they are not washed away by the tide.

• A freshwater swamp is formed from a shallow lake surrounded by plants. As leaves and flowers fall into the water, a layer of ooze builds up. The ooze slowly accumulates to form a swamp.

• The world's largest swamp is the Gran Pantanal in Brazil. It covers an area that is about the same size as the state of Tennessee.

Swamp cypress
The swamp cypress grows in the freshwater swamps of the southern American states. It has spongy breathing roots that stick up above the waterlogged ground. Air enters the roots and spreads to the parts below the surface.

Life in a swamp

The swirling, muddy water of a mangrove swamp is home to kingfishers, giant water bugs, turtles, crocodiles, and mud skippers.

Support roots

The *Rhizophora* mangrove tree supports itself on prop roots that absorb oxygen from the air. Unwanted salt from seawater is taken in through its roots and stored in special leaves that fall off when they are full.

Breathing roots

The *Avicennia* mangrove has breathing roots that grow upward. Their tips are above the surface when muddy water covers the main roots.

AMAZING TREES

HAVE you ever seen any strange or peculiar looking trees? Some trees may look strange, but they need to be this way in order to survive. For example, a baobab tree uses its bloated trunk to store water for the dry season. Other trees are amazing because of size. Trees grow throughout their lives, so a very old tree can be a very big tree. Some of the oldest and most massive living trees are the redwood trees of California that can grow to over 300 feet (90 m) high. Trees grow outward as well as upward. A banyan tree in India has spread to almost 1/4 mile (.4 km) across.

This miniature tree is fully grown. It is the result of the Japanese art of tree pruning, called bonsai. Over many years, its roots and shoots have been carefully cut to limit its growth.

Fossilized trees
These tree trunks were alive millions of years ago. They sank into the ground and were slowly changed into stony fossils. Wind and rain uncovered them, and they now lie on the surface of the Algerian desert in North Africa.

FACT BOX

• A giant wellingtonia, a type of redwood, weighs as much as 100 railroad locomotives.

• A fig tree in Calcutta Botanic Gardens, in India, has a canopy 400 feet (122 m) across. It almost covers two football fields.

• Some coco-de-mer tree nuts weigh over 500 pounds (227 kilograms) each.

• A wild fig tree at Echo Caves in South Africa has roots 350 feet (107 m) deep.

Giant redwoods
California redwood trees (*left*) take over 2,000 years to grow 300 feet (90 m) high and can weigh over 6,000 tons (5,445 metric tons). Their enormous size is shown by these nine-year-olds standing beside a typical redwood trunk (*right*).

Sack-of-potatoes tree

The very strange sack-of-potatoes tree has rounded dents in its trunk that make it look like a tummy. It also is called the desert rose because it blooms with pink flowers in winter. Its swollen trunk stores water.

Cucumber tree

The amazing cucumber tree also stores water in its thick trunk. It can survive extreme droughts by shedding all its leaves. The tree then stays dormant and protected until rain arrives.

Traveler's palm

The traveler's palm can provide thirsty people with a drink. It grows in hot countries. If a hole is made at the bottom of the stalk, where the leaf joins the trunk, refreshing watery sap spurts out.

LEAF FALL, DEATH, & DECAY

As autumn comes, trees prepare for winter. Delicate leaves would be harmed by cold winter winds, so the trees take back their food and seal the leaves off at the base. The leaves change color and fall to the ground. All these colorful leaves have died, but they still are vital for the life of the trees above. As they lie on the ground, they start to rot. Tiny living creatures, called decomposers, use them for food. Decomposers include microscopic bacteria, fungi, insects, and other tiny animals. They digest the leaves and break them down, releasing nutrients the trees must have for growth in the coming spring. Life, death, and decay are linked in an endless cycle.

A beech forest in the fall. The leaves dry out and turn golden yellow. Food and sap flow back into the trees, and the leaves fill with unwanted substances. The joints between the stalks and twigs loosen, and the leaves fall.

Decomposers
Dead leaves are food for decomposers such as wood lice. They eat the fallen leaves and pass many of the nutrients back into the soil to be taken up again by the trees' roots.

Leaf skeleton
The thinnest part of a leaf is digested by decomposers first. The stalk, midrib, and veins are the toughest parts. They form a skeleton that may take a year or more to be broken down.

48

The death of a tree

Toward the end of its life, a tree is invaded by decomposers, especially fungi. Fungi feed on the dead and living wood. Dead branches fall off as the wood is weakened. Finally, the trunk topples to the ground and rots away.

Leaves fall.

Tree rotters

About 15 years after this tree fell, its stump is steadily decaying. Tunneling insects have loosened the bark. Toadstools sprout from the tendrils of fungi that reach right through the stump as they digest the wood to a soggy pulp.

Nutrients dissolve in rainwater and sink into the soil.

Recycled life

Trees need nutrients from the soil to grow. These nutrients come from dead and rotting leaves, trees, and animals. Fungi, microscopic bacteria, and tiny animals break down the rotting material and recycle the nutrients back into the soil.

Dead leaves lie on the ground.

Fungi and animals decompose, or break down, the leaves.

LIFE IN THE LEAF LITTER

You will need: plastic soda bottles (one large and one small), scissors, gloves, plastic funnel, damp soil, sand, about 6 worms, damp rotting leaves, black paper.

I N the fall, piles of leaves litter the ground. Slowly, they rot away, until it seems there is nothing left. Rotting does not happen by itself. The decomposers – millions of fungi, microscopic bacteria, and tiny creatures – eat away at the leaves and break them down. Decomposers digest leaves and turn them into nutrients. These nutrients are important chemicals that dissolve in rainwater and trickle down to the tree roots below. Living trees need these recycled nutrients in order to grow. Earthworms work as decomposers. Make a wormery, and you will see how worms pull dead leaves into their underground tunnels. You also can separate decomposers from the rotting leaves they live in with a lamp, a funnel, and a jar.

Make a wormery

1 Cut the top off the large bottle, *as shown*. Place the small bottle inside the large one. Make sure the gap between the bottles is spaced evenly all the way around.

Worm burrowing

2 Wear gloves and use a funnel to fill the gap with layers of soil and sand, patted down, to within 3 inches (7.5 cm) of the top. Add worms, covered with dead leaves.

3 Cover the wormery with black paper. Keep the soil moist. The worms will soon tunnel away from the light and drag leaves with them. Return the worms to the wild.

Studying decomposers

You will need: plastic funnel, large clear jar, gloves, rotting leaves from a compost heap, damp tissue, black paper, desk lamp, magnifying glass, field guide.

1 Dead leaves are full of insects and other creatures. Separate them by using a lamp, a funnel, and a jar. Put the funnel inside the jar, *as shown*.

2 Wearing gloves, fill the funnel loosely with dead leaves. Put damp tissue in the bottom of the jar. Wrap black paper around the jar to block out the light.

3 Place the desk lamp so that it shines on the leaves. The animals will move away from the heat and light of the lamp and fall down the slippery funnel into the jar below.

4 After an hour, there will be several animals in the jar. Look at them with a magnifying glass and use a field guide to identify them. When you have finished, return the animals to where you found them.

PREHISTORIC TREES

This is the fossilized imprint of a leaf, 50 million years old. The leaf was buried in mud that turned to stone. Splitting open the stone shows where the leaf left its mark.

OAK, eucalyptus, redwood, and baobab – have these trees always grown on earth? Scientists think that trees were very different millions of years ago. Fossils dug up by paleontologists, or scientists who study fossils, tell us that the earliest trees grew about 350 million years ago. This was long before the dinosaurs first lived on earth about 200 million years ago, or the first modern humans appeared just 1 million years ago. The earliest treelike plants looked a lot like bunches of feathery ferns growing at the top of a woody trunk. As time went by, these ancient trees gradually changed to suit the world as it changed. Trees that did not suit the environment became extinct, or died out. About 135 million years ago, the first trees with blossoms appeared on earth. Some trees today, such as the waxy-petaled magnolia, look very much like these early flowering trees.

How coal formed

Coal is called a fossil fuel. It was formed about 300 million years ago when many trees grew in steamy swamps. Dead trees fell into the stagnant muddy water. The water was too foul for decomposers to live in, so the wood did not rot away.

Soggy layers of vegetation – trees, leaves, and other plants – all piled up on top of each other. Over millions of years, rivers dumped enormous amounts of mud and silt on top of them. The weight above compressed the vegetation into a solid mass.

Hundreds of yards (meters) below the surface, underground heat broke down chemicals in the buried vegetation. Everything slowly fossilized and turned solid. Trees and other vegetation became coal (the black layers) and mud became layers of rock as labeled.

Carboniferous period

The Carboniferous period was about 350 to 280 million years ago. Forests of giant ferns and trees like shaggy palms grew in vast swamps. Large amphibians and many insects thrived in the swamps.

Gingko leaves
One of the oldest surviving species of trees is the gingko, which first grew over 200 million years ago.

Cretaceous period

The Cretaceous period was about 140 to 65 million years ago. Many conifers were growing, and flowering deciduous trees appeared. Dinosaurs roamed across the land but died out by the end of this period.

Tertiary period

The Tertiary period was about 65 to 5 million years ago. Flowering deciduous trees became common. Mammals quickly took over after the dinosaurs died out.

WOOD AS A MATERIAL

How many objects around you are made of wood? There are tables and chairs. Houses have wood floors held up by wood beams, and the roofs are supported by wooden rafters. Trees that have been cut down to make things are called timber. There are two kinds of timber – softwood and hardwood. Softwood comes from fast-growing conifers, such as pines and firs. Hardwood comes from slower-growing, broad-leaved trees, such as oaks and maples. Planks are made by sawing tree trunks along their lengths. Larger sheets of plywood are made by shaving trunks into layers and gluing the layers together.

Many objects are made of wood, such as chairs and tables, paper, envelopes, books, and pencils.

Chipboard is made from sawdust and flakes of waste wood mixed with glue. Sheets of chipboard are up to 8 feet (2.5 m) wide, far wider than most tree trunks. Flooring and furniture can be made of chipboard.

Timber forests
This forester is cutting down a 60-year-old pine tree. The tree's side branches and thin tops will be cut away, leaving a long straight trunk, which will be much easier to transport to the sawmill.

Sawmills
In the sawmill, machines rip off the bark, and huge saws cut the trunk into planks. Timber must be seasoned, or dried out, before it can be used.

Carving wood

The main part of this American Indian totem pole is made from a single tree trunk. Knives, axes, and chisels are used to carve the wood into all sorts of different shapes and patterns.

Wooden sailing ships

This is a reconstruction of the *Mayflower*, the ship that took the Pilgrims from England to North America in 1620. It took hundreds of trees to build a wooden sailing ship. Oak trees were used to build the main hull. Pine trees were used for the deck planks.

Log rollers

About 4,500 years ago, the Egyptians built pyramids from huge blocks of stone. They probably moved the blocks on wood sledges dragged along on rollers made of tree trunks.

CHEMICALS FROM TREES

JUST like you, and everything else in the universe, trees are made from chemicals. Trees take in simple chemicals from the ground and from the air. They use these substances and energy from the sun to make complicated chemicals. Many of these chemicals are useful in our world. Some are found in the leaves, fruits, or bark of trees. Many other chemicals are made by heating wood in huge ovens. The ovens are airtight, so the wood does not burn. Heat boils the liquid chemicals out of the wood and changes them into gases. Cooling the gases makes a liquid mixture that then can be separated into different chemicals.

Rubber in car tires comes from trees. Sap called latex flows from cuts made in the bark of rubber trees. The latex is collected and processed to make rubber.

Eucalyptus leaves

Aspirin

Natural painkiller
Tree bark contains many chemicals. The bark of willow trees can be used as a painkiller and to reduce fever. It was the original source of the drug aspirin. Today, aspirin is made from chemicals found in crude oil.

Willow bark

Eucalyptus oil

Medicinal leaves
Eucalyptus trees have oil in their leaves. The leaves are heated with steam to drive out the oil. It has a pleasant smell and is used to clear a stuffed-up nose.

Turpentine

This artist is using oil paints. She is making them thinner and more runny by adding turpentine. This liquid is one of the main chemicals made by heating wood in an airtight oven.

Tanning hide

Animal skins are stiff until they are softened by tanning. In the tanning process, the skins are soaked in a mixture of bark chips and water. The chemicals in the bark help soften the skins.

FACT BOX

• Rosewood oil, steamed from the trunks of trees that grow in rain forests, is used in perfumes, cosmetics, and flavorings.

• Quinine, first extracted from the bark of the South American cinchona tree, is used to treat a deadly illness called malaria.

• Gamboge is a brilliant yellow dye made from the sap of the Indian garcinia tree. It is used to dye the robes of Buddhist monks.

• Curare comes from the bark of a South American tree. Doctors use it to relax the muscles of patients during operations.

• The sap of the Central American chicle tree is an ingredient in chewing gum.

• Sticky resin from pine trees is used in glue, medicine, ink, perfume, and insecticide.

Polished wood

Wood can look more beautiful by polishing it regularly. Polish puts a protective layer on the surface of the wood. The waxes and resins used in polish come from the chemicals given off by heating wood.

POLLUTION AND DESTRUCTION

EVERYTHING we do seems to have a hidden cost. Think of all the fuels we burn – coal to generate electricity, gas for cooking and heating, and gas and diesel oil in cars and trucks. Burning fuels creates pollution. Two results of pollution are the greenhouse effect, which causes the earth to warm up, and acid rain, which poisons our world. Many people eat hamburgers which destroys forests, because hamburger meat comes from cattle that eat grass. Ranchers in South America cut down rain forests to plant the grass. Without these forests, heavy rain beats straight onto the ground and washes away the soil.

A tree damaged by acid rain. The acid rain strips the leaves of their protective coating of wax. The result is disease, usually followed by death.

FACT BOX

• About 37 million acres (15 million hectares) of rain forest are cut down each year.

• A total of 70 acres (28 ha) of forest is cleared every minute. It takes at least 150 years for forest to regrow on cleared land.

• Only 12 caoba trees are left in the wild, in the jungles of Ecuador, South America.

• Each year, fuels burned in Great Britain pour about 6 million tons (5.4 million metric tons) of acid gases into the air.

Acid rain
Polluting gases from power stations and vehicles rise into the air. The gases join with oxygen and water from the air and change into acid. The wind carries the pollution, far from where it was made, to fall as acid rain.

Destroying the rain forest

Every year, large areas of rain forest are cut down for timber. The ground is cleared by burning to make way for crops and grazing. Rain forest soil is very low in nutrients. Without the trees, it soon is exhausted and can be farmed only for a short time.

Deforestation

Tree roots hold the soil in place. Leaves absorb the force of falling rain. When forests are cut down, soil is washed away. Rushing water causes flooding, and exposed earth turns to desert.

Habitat loss

Many forest animals, like this sloth, are in danger of dying out because their habitats, or homes, are being cut down. These animals depend on trees and plants for food and places to live.

Greenhouse effect

The burning of fuels releases carbon dioxide gas into the atmosphere. Carbon dioxide lets the sun's rays pass through the atmosphere but traps some of the heat, much like the glass in a greenhouse. This effect is steadily making the earth's climate warmer.

Sun

Atmosphere lets in sun's rays

Some heat is reflected back

Earth warms up

CONSERVATION

If you have room in your yard or at school, replant your living Christmas tree. Get a tree with healthy, long roots. When the festivities are over and the weather warms, plant the tree outside.

How important do you think trees are? From reading this book, you know that trees are very important. They change carbon dioxide gas in the air back into oxygen for people and animals to breathe. They provide food, fuel, timber, and chemicals. They keep the soil healthy and provide homes and food for countless living things. Trees shade living things from the sun, and they are beautiful to the eye. We should take care of trees and make sure our woods and forests do not disappear. Humans have exploited trees for many years – we chop them down without thinking of the future. We now should do our best to conserve, or protect, trees and use them wisely. We need trees for the future, so we must get busy planning and planting them today.

Replanting
A specialized machine plants young fir seedlings in the ground. The young seedlings are grown in a nursery as stock for replanting forests. As forests are cut down for their timber, new trees are planted.

FACT BOX

• The world's oldest national park is Yellowstone in the United States, established in 1872. Banff National Park in Canada was set up in 1887, although coal mining and tree felling did not stop until 1923. Just over 5 percent of the world's land now is protected.

• If you attend your first school for six years, there is just enough time for you to grow seedlings, plant a hedge, and watch it grow to your own height before you leave.

• The United Nations Food and Agriculture Organization (FAO) was set up to teach people new ways of farming so they do not harm the land.

Forest fires

Bush fires in Australia destroy trees each year. Large forests have firebreaks, which are wide roadways with no trees. The firebreaks help stop fire from spreading.

Protected areas

Yellowstone National Park is pictured *above*. Many countries have set aside woods and forests as conservation areas or national parks. Wild creatures and plants reside there with as little interference as possible from humans.

Coppice wood

Coppicing is a good way to make use of woodland resources. These shoots *(above)* have grown from the stumps of hazel trees. Every few years, the shoots are harvested and used for fuel or timber.

Recycling

Paper is made from wood chippings. One tree makes enough paper for only 400 copies of an ordinary newspaper. You can help conserve trees by recycling old newspapers. Waste paper is mixed with wood chippings to make new paper.

MAKE A TREE MUSEUM

By now, you know a great deal about trees. Why not use your knowledge to make a tree museum for your friends to enjoy? Collect some leaves, bark, buds, cattails, and flowers, as well as fruits, seeds, and cones. You also can make rubbings of bark and leaves. Do not forget to look for items throughout the year – flowers and buds in the spring, seeds and fruits in the fall. To complete your collection, cut pictures out of old magazines. Keep everything in shoe boxes until you can display them. Label your collection and note any interesting facts. Use pictures and drawings to make posters to hang on the wall.

When collecting items for your museum, make sure you have permission to take them away. Be thoughtful, tidy, organized, and safe. Always wear gloves when handling items.

Here is some of the equipment you might find useful to study trees and the creatures that live on them. Build up your stock of equipment along with your collection.

field guide

large glass jar

containers

plastic magnifier

paper

scissors

plastic bags

adhesive labels

magnifying glass

paintbrush

camera

colored pencils

gloves

pencil

notebook

Collecting specimens

1 How many different kinds of leaves can you find? Identify them using a field guide. Look at pages 18 and 19 for information to help you sort out and store your collection. Make sure you note the name of the tree each leaf comes from.

2 Collect only bark from dead trees that have fallen over. You can make bark rubbings of living trees. See page 15 for instructions on how to do this.

3 Springtime flowers soon wither and die. These young horse chestnuts will last much longer. Rather than picking flowers, it is better to take photos of them.

4 You can look at young cones and leaves on the lowest branches of evergreen pines, firs, and cedars. Look under these trees for cones that have fallen.

5 Start arranging your museum. You can make a display case from a shoe box by sticking in pieces of cardboard to make individual compartments. Work with friends to make a large display to help people learn about trees and how we must care for them.

GLOSSARY

algae – microscopic plants with no roots, stems, or leaves that cluster together by the millions and grow mostly in water and damp places.

anther – a male part of a flower that makes the pollen needed for the plant to reproduce.

bonsai – a potted tree or shrub that has been carefully cut and trimmed to keep it a certain shape and small size.

buttress roots – roots that grow up the sides of some very tall trees and flare out at the bottom to keep the tree upright.

Carboniferous period – a time in the development of the earth, hundreds of millions of years ago, when the land was mostly big swamps, where large animals and insects lived, and the forests were mostly big plants, like giant ferns.

chlorophyll – the green coloring in the leaves of plants that is needed to absorb the sun's energy.

coniferous – describes the kinds of trees and shrubs that have needle-like leaves that do not fall off in the cold seasons and that grow their seeds inside of cones instead of flowers.

conservation – taking care of natural resources by using them wisely, protecting them, and replacing them.

cotyledon – the part of a plant seed that provides food for the embryo that will grow into a root or a shoot of a new plant.

Cretaceous period – a time in the development of the earth, about a hundred million years ago, when the land became layers of ground and rock, where trees and flowering plants appeared, and during which the dinosaurs lived and gradually disappeared.

deciduous – describes the kinds of trees and shrubs that have broad, flat, green leaves that fall off at the end of the growing season and that grow their seeds inside of flowers, fruits, and nuts.

decomposers – microscopic bacteria, fungi, insects, or other tiny creatures that eat dead leaves and other dead parts of plants and animals, turning them into nutrients in the soil.

decomposition – the process in which dead plants and animals decay, breaking down into other natural materials or chemical elements.

drupe – a fruit, like a peach, plum, or cherry, that has juicy flesh and a large stone or pit in the middle with a seed inside it.

embryo – the tiny plant inside a seed that grows into a new plant.

fossil fuel – a type of fuel that comes from the ground, like coal, which was formed from dead trees and other vegetation that did not decompose.

fungus (*pl.* fungi) – plants, like mushrooms and molds, that do not have chlorophyll and cannot make their own food.

germinate – to begin to develop a sprout or a bud.

glucose – the sugar that forms in a plant during photosynthesis. It is used by the plant for food to grow.

osmosis – the process in which a fluid gradually passes through a layer of tissue, or membrane, (as if it is being absorbed) into a thicker, or more concentrated, substance on the other side to make the concentration of fluid on both sides of the membrane equal.

ovules – tiny female parts within the flower or cone of a plant or tree that, when joined with pollen made by the male parts of the flower or cone, develop into seeds that will grow into new plants or trees.

paleontologist – a scientist who studies fossils.

phloem – a delicate layer of wood underneath the bark of a tree through which dissolved food is carried to other parts of the tree.

photosynthesis – the process by which green plants use energy from the sun to turn water and carbon dioxide into glucose (a simple sugar) for food, releasing oxygen into the air for people and animals to breathe.

pillar roots – roots that grow down from the lower limbs of a tree with very wide-spreading branches and take root in the ground to support the tree's top and help it spread over a wide area.

pip – the small seed in fruits, such as apples.

pollination – the process by which pollen from the anthers (male parts) of a plant is moved to the ovules (female parts) of the plant to make seeds.

prop roots – roots that grow out of the trunk of some trees that have tall, thin stems. They anchor themselves in the ground, like tent ropes, to support the tree.

stigma – the female part of a flower, attached to the ovule, that catches the pollen the ovule needs to become a seed.

stoma (*pl*. stomata) – one of many microscopic holes on the underside of a plant's leaves through which carbon dioxide moves in and oxygen moves out during the process of photosynthesis.

Tertiary period – a time in the development of the earth, less than a hundred million years ago, when the land, plants, and animals were more like the ones known today.

transpiration – the process in which sunshine turns liquid water in the leaves of plants into water vapor that escapes into the air through holes on the undersides of the leaves. The water vapor gathers in the air, and, when it is cooled, it turns back into liquid water.

xylem vessels – the tubelike tissue in the stems and trunks of plants and trees through which water is drawn upward into the plant.

BOOKS

The Blossom on the Bough: A Book of Trees.
Anne O. Dowden (Ticknor & Fields Books
for Young Readers)

Forests. Under the Microscope (series).
John Woodward (Gareth Stevens)

*How Monkeys Make Chocolate: Foods and Medicines
from the Rainforests.* Adrian Forsyth
(Firefly Books)

*Inside the Amazing Amazon: Incredible Fold-Out
Cross Sections of the World's Greatest Rain forests.*
Don Lessem (Crown Publishing Group)

*The Nature and Science of Leaves. Exploring the Science
of Nature (series).* Jane Burton and Kim Taylor
(Gareth Stevens)

Nature's Green Umbrella: Tropical Rain Forests.
Gail Gibbons (Morrow)

Protecting Our Forests. Rosa Costa-Pace
(Chelsea House)

*The Remarkable Rain forests: An Active-Learning
Book for Kids.* Toni Albert (Trickle Creek)

Temperate Deciduous Forest. April P. Sayre
(TFC Books)

Timber: From Trees to Wood Products.
William Jaspersohn (Little, Brown)

The Tree Almanac: A Year-Round Activity Guide.
Monica Russo (Sterling)

Young Naturalist Field Guides. (Gareth Stevens)

VIDEOS

The Changing Forests: A First Film.
(Phoenix/BFA Films and Video)

A First Look at Trees. (AIMS Media)

*The Life of a Forest (series). The Birth of a Forest.
A Forest Grows Old.* (United Learning, Inc.)

Photosynthesis. (AIMS Media)

Seeds in Motion. (Pyramid Media)

Temperate and Deciduous Forest. (MBG Videos)

Trees: Evergreens and Deciduous. (AIMS Media)

WEB SITES

www.domtar.com/arbre/english

www.nationalgeographic.com

Some web sites stay current longer than others. For further web sites, use your search engines to
locate the following topics: *forestry, leaves, photosynthesis, pollination, pollution, tree conservation.*

INDEX

RECEIVED

AUG 2 8 2000

WALNUT CREEK
SCHOOL DISTRICT

ght
gden/Bruce Coleman Ltd: 24br; Hans Reinhard/Bruce Coleman Ltd: 27cl. Sally Morgan/Ecoscene: 17tr; Nick
Ecoscene: 17bl. Bob Gibbons/Holt Studios: 13tr, 13br; Inga Spence/Holt Studios: 27bl, 31bl; Irene Lengui/Holt
45br; Richard Anthony/Holt Studios: 46c; Duncan Smith/Holt Studios: 49bl; Nigel Cattlin/Holt Studios: 24bl,
l; Willem Harinck/Holt Studios: 60bl. Nature Photographers Ltd: 8b, 9tl, 14bc, 15br, 21tr, 31tr, 32bc, 42bl, 52tl.
rupaker Senani/Oxford Scientific Films: 13tl; Richard Bailey/Oxford Scientific Films: 22tr; Edward Parker/
Scientific Films: 43br; Zig Leszcynski: 46bl; Breck P. Kent/Oxford Scientific Films 54br. Planet Earth
3tc. Tony Stone Worldwide: 55l, 59bl. Zefa Pictures: pages 4c, 13bl, 17tr, 31tl, 38bc, 41br, 42 br, 44br,